I AM AMIDST YOU NOW

GOD THE F...
HEALING MY TRUTH

PENNY MCCOY

STRATTON
—PRESS—
Publishing Life

I AM AMIDST YOU NOW
Copyright © 2018 **Penny McCoy**

Stratton Press, LLC
1603 Capitol Ave, Suite 310,
Cheyenne, WY 82001
www.stratton-press.com
1-888-323-7009

ISBN (Paperback): 978-1-64345-015-5
ISBN (Ebook): 978-1-64345-168-8

Illustrations by Summer Thompson

Printed in the United States of America

DEDICATION

I dedicate this book to the heart of God as our Father and to your hearts, His children.

My intention is for this book to be used as a tool to set your heart free, positioning your heart for healing and wholeness so you can be released into the destiny God has spoken for your life from eternity past, to eternity present, into eternity future.

You are the creation of His pleasure. He delights in the greatness, completeness, and joy of you as you carry out the destiny of His plans. His plans are always for a hopeful, abundant life where you receive the revelation of His heart and live His heart to your fullest potential.

God's heart always makes known to you the path of life. His heart fills you with joy in His presence. It gives you eternal pleasures as you live your life in the destiny of His plans in partnership with His gracious strength and wisdom.

It is my hope that each person who reads this book will be used as God the Father's vessel for such a time as this to share His glory to the outer ends of the earth.

Inasmuch as this is my hope, I dedicate this book ultimately to the glory of God and His mighty power at work within us as His children.

I Am amidst you now
My miracles to perform
I Am not dead
I Am alive and I Am yours to behold

CONTENTS

INTRODUCTION

You must know the words in this book are not my words or just a good idea. They are messages from the heart of God as our Father to our hearts, His children. They are written from the perspective of God's heavenly point of view down to us, not our point of view up to Him.

My intention is for this book to be a testimony about the true Light of the world. It is also an acknowledgement that in Him, there is no darkness or shadow of turning.

This is the age of the face-off between the darkness and the Light. The Light does shine in the darkness and extinguish its power. It always has, and it always will. The darkness has not understood the Light; however, the Light is still God, and God is still the Light the darkness succumbs to.

Even though the darkness surrounds us, the darkness cannot hide from the Light's true promise.

> The eye is the lamp of the body.
> If your eyes are good,
> Your whole body will be full of *light*.
>
> But if your eyes are bad,
> Your whole body will be full of darkness.
>
> If then *the light* within you is darkness,
> How great is that darkness.
>
> (Matt. 6:22–23)

Make no mistake! We cannot hide!

SECTION ONE

This is the day God's voice is going to be heard upon the earth above the voice of the darkness, the enemy of our soul, our self-centered will, fear, pride, envy, jealousy, bitterness, rejection, anger, justification, the manipulations of religion, the traditions or approval of man, control, abuse, injustice, or any lofty thing exalting itself above the knowledge of God.

God's spirit is moving in the earth today, performing miracles and signs that make people wonder. The hand of man won't be able to stay the hand of God during these times. God is drawing each of us face-to-face with himself, where we have to give an answer for our own lives, not point the finger at others in an attempt to use the blame we cast as a justification for compromise.

This is a time where the rubber will meet the road and accountability will be the road we travel. We are individually being challenged to work out our own salvation with a healthy fear and trembling, recognizing it is what God the Son has done and accomplished for us, His children.

This is a period in history when we are faced with relentless deception. The darkness will be distinguished from the Light as the east is from the west. As the darkness grows expeditiously darker, the Light will burn brighter on the horizon of God's prophetic vision for the world at large.

It is vital that we listen to the voice of God and obey what He speaks. That is the only right thing to do. And as we do the right thing, our fruit will be the peace, rest, strength, and confidence we need to live in the land He has for us to inherit.

Listen to the voice of God. Obey the voice of God, and live in safety. Trust in what He says, and be at ease without fear of harm.

God is wooing our hearts as His children into a divine, intimate relationship second to none. His destiny for our lives must reign supreme. Compromise will chill our soul as never before and take more than we ever want to give.

These messages are, in a fashion, Psalms for such a time as this. They are to be used to help free His captive children today. He led His captive children out of Egypt in Old Testament times, and He sets free those today who choose to love Him more than anyone or anything else that holds them captive to anything but His will.

As God sets a portion of your heart free, He positions that portion for healing and wholeness. Once the healing and wholeness has taken place in that area of your heart, there is a release to receive His destiny in that area.

God yearns for us to be set free and delivered from our issues. When that happens, we can move on in Him and be all that He created us be and do all He created us to do.

We are His masterpiece. He has spoken from the beginning of time good things for us to do and accomplish. God has a plan and we all fit into it. The question is, will we choose to fit into it?

I believe these messages will tug on heartstrings and question resolve. Perhaps they will take us to a place where that place might become the end of ourselves in certain areas. They may challenge the very essence of who we are, what we think, and what we deem important in the scheme of eternity. They hold within them the possibility to challenge our intention within the framework of our motivation, will, and emotions. We will have to choose many times whom we will serve in these final hours.

God is not mocked. He is not afraid of a good fight, and He always wins. Which side are you on? Are you fighting the good fight of faith, or has *compromise* chilled your soul?

SECTION TWO

Contained in this section are messages, exposition, expression, and illustrations depicting God's heart as our Father. They represent the grace-filled, loving, and faithful beauty of His heart to our hearts, His children.

I believe these messages will encourage souls, uplift eyes, challenge hearts, nurture minds, soothe wounds, exalt truth, contend for freedom, and offer hope to destiny.

I believe God's heart stimulates thinking, confronts compromise, births possibilities, gives rise to the greatness of God, and expands the horizon of all that we are.

God's heart salutes the truth and does damage to the lie that He is dead, silent, or anything we want in order to fit Him into compromising, self-willed lifestyles.

These messages are the inspiration of the Holy Spirit of God. It is my hope they renew and water seeds of healing, deliverance, wholeness, and freedom.

God's Spirit draws our spirits to the crossroads of life. His instructions give opportunity for us to discover we have to choose which path we travel each turn of the way. You and I are no different! You can win or lose! It's up to you!

God's messages confirm that God himself is amidst us now, healing His truth to this lost and dying world. His truth is, He is not dead. He's alive and risen! He has ears that hear, eyes that see, a voice that speaks, and all authority and power to make nations tremble.

God knows everything that is and is not hidden. He knows every heart. He knows every need. He's the reality of and the conduit to heaven. He knows the end from the beginning, and He is the beginning and the end.

I AM AMIDST YOU NOW
HEALING MY TRUTH

Do you know
I Am amidst you now
Healing my truth
To this lost and dying world

My children, I Am that I Am amidst you now and always will be. I Am that I Am forever and always the same. Time has attempted to erase my face, and the human heart has sought other ways, but I Am the way, the truth, and the life. There is no other true God.

Lies last for the moment. Deception takes your breath away. The freedom I came and died to give supersedes the chains of bondage that have you enslaved.

Can't you see the understanding of the world isn't mine at all? The understanding of the world handcuffs your heart. It has nothing to do with me. The understanding of my heart establishes heaven in your midst.

Isn't fear the thing that you placate when there's only fear to rely on? And what else do you have to lean on if your leaning isn't on me? For I Am that I Am and I came to set you free. How can freedom ring if you fear life itself and the very air you breathe?

What do your ears hear, my children, be you young or old? Do your ears hear hope, or are they encapsulated within this lost and dying world? You can hear my voice if you choose. I Am that I Am and my voice is always that it is.

My voice is the gentle whisper in the storm and the peaceful eye of your hurricane as it blows. It is the Son, Spirit, and Father all in one. It is my ever-present help in time of need.

I Am the voice, and I Am He. Listen to me speak. Pay attention to what I say. Listen carefully. Don't lose sight of my words. Allow the revelation of my words to penetrate the innermost sanctum of your heart. They will bring gifts of life and radiant health if you discover their meaning.

Tune your ears to the sound of my direction. Listen to my direction speak. Hold it closely. Tightly wrap it in the arms of the purity of your heart. Don't let go of my instructions. Carry them out for I Am amidst you now, telling you of my tender mercies, offering you my love, and healing my truth to this lost and dying world.

Are you careful, my children, what forms on your tongue? Is your mouth cherished with wisdom pouring life out? Do you speak of my unfailing love so that young and old may know that I Am amidst them now, my miracles to perform?

Do you share my faithfulness to this needy world? Are you captured with the grandeur of yourself when I Am the one you are supposed to partake of and depend upon?

Are you on the throne ruled by your ego and impressed with your strength and figuring? Are you "You are that you are," or am I "I Am that I Am"?

Are you releasing your plans into my hands so your destiny can be uncovered? Are you thinking of me and allowing me to lead? If you do, you can be set free to become all you are meant to be, and your life can become the masterpiece that I speak.

I Am amidst you now healing my truth, disheveling the lie of false gods. Lies last for the moment. My truth fails not. I Am the truth and the only way. I Am the truth now and always.

I Am abundant life and provide all you'll ever need. What you believe changes that not. Will you partake, or will you not?

I Am amidst you now healing my truth. Will you humble yourself and trust me as God?

I Am amidst you now my children
Healing my truth

Do you not know
I surround you with my spirit
And my truth to unfold
You are sheltered beneath my wings
And enraptured in me
Can't you see
I Am amidst you now
My miracles to perform

Don't you know
It is me that shows you all things

Can you touch my face
And hope in my love

I Am amidst you now
Even in you if you please

Put me first in thought and word
Share my faithfulness
To the needy dying world

Put me on the throne
Come without delay
My miracles are waiting
For you to display my splendor and my grace

Oh my children don't you know
I Am amidst you now
Healing my truth
To this lost and dying world

Lies last for a time
The truth lasts forever and forever is mine

Recognize
I Am amidst you now come to set you free

Wait no more
Come I beckon you come
I Am the one you need

My children I Am amidst you now
My angels I release

The crown of thorns on my head
The sweat on my brow
The lashes on my back
And the cross that I bore
All say to you
I won't ever leave you nor will I forsake
I Am in heaven
And I Am here for you to partake

Sing of my tender mercies
Walk in my unfailing love
Take hold of my freedom
That young and old may know
I Am amidst them now
Healing my truth
And performing miracles on their behalf

Lies last for a moment
Truth stands the test of time

I Am eternal
I Am not the lie

I Am that I Am
I Am not compromise

This is the age of tolerance
Although tolerance to the wrong thing
Will put your soul in a vice
And your heart in the grave
Your mind will think it is hiding
but I will know where it lies

Seek everything else
All your other gods
You won't find them alive
When you are on your way out
You won't find they have risen
They could not come out of their graves
They aren't the ones with power to save

Come be free
Come seek my face and you will see...

I AM THE ETERNAL TIME CLOCK
INCHING AWAY TIME

I Am that I Am
And I Am forever and always I have been

I Am forever and always
And always I will be
I Am forever and forever is me

My children, I Am forever, and forever is me. I Am eternity present, eternity past, and forever eternity inching away time.

I Am forever the Father and always the Son and eternally my Spirit, and we are always one.

I Am forever the truth and always have been.

I Am forever your freedom and always will be.

I Am forever my presence and my presence is me.

I Am forever and always will be the hands of your destiny.

Fight me you may, but you won't win. Time is on my side. Won't you join in?

I Am amidst you now proving time within the boundaries of my voice and the very heart of God.

I Am amidst you now healing my truth and bringing each of you to the end of yourself. As you come to the end of yourself, questions will arise.

Do you hold time in your hands, or is it mine?

Have you gone up to heaven and come down as God?

Have you gathered the wind in the hollow of your fists or wrapped the waters of the universe in your cloak?

Have you established all the ends of the earth?

Is it your glory others need to see?

Are all your words flawless and what the world needs?

Are you the shield my children can use for protection?

Are you the shelter for the molested?

Are you the truth that can set a heart free, and is it your power that heals and saves eternally? No. I Am He. I hold all things of life forever, now and always.

It is time you recognize I Am time and forever time is me. I Am the Savior, and the Savior is me.

You are not the clock at the right hand of my Father's throne. I Am and I alone. I Am forever the eternal time clock ticking away time.

I Am ebbing and flowing. I Am kind. I Am calling and wooing you to my side. It's time you submit to the abundance I Am.

It is time you doubt not my wisdom and shame not my grace. Look not to the watch and its hands so fine. Rather look to me when you are blind. In me you'll find praise for my plan and praise for my design.

I Am the eternal time clock
You must do that moment as I speak
Not a minute too soon
Certainly not ever so late

Belabor me not
Pain my heart no more
Hurt me less more and more

My children doubt not my wisdom
Shame not my grace
Heed my voice at the moment it speaks

I Am the eternal time clock
Inching away time
Ebbing and flowing at my Father's pace
I Am the eternal time clock
On the plan of life

I Am the eternal time clock
You are not to interrupt

Do not offer up foolishness
That I be disdained
Do not offer up foolishness
At the outset of my grace

Praise me for my design
Praise me for my plan
Praise me for my time
It is your gain

I Am the eternal time clock
Worry not yours ticking on

Be not guided by the natural ticking
Of its hands so fine

I Am the eternal time clock
It's in me you'll find
Purpose and fulfillment and my guiding light

Be not mistaken
Do not be late nor too soon
Follow my clock and its movement
It is eternal and perfectly in sync with my plan

I Am the eternal time clock
Inching away time
Every moment matters
Give them respect

The secret is I Am eternity and eternity is me

The question is do I live in you
And do you live in me
If so eternally we will be linked

Know that time is ticking
And won't ever wait
Make the most of your time here on earth
Eternity is at stake

I Am the eternal time clock
Ticking away time
Live as if you are not blind
Live as if a minute is too late
A second is too soon
If it isn't what I direct

Live as if you know
Once you breathe your last breath
There will be eternity in store

But where

I Am amidst you now healing my truth
That I Am forever and won't go away
I Am forever and my plan won't be erased

Each moment as it leaves won't ever come again
Make the most of now
Before now is over and you're faced with the end

I Am that I Am and I Am eternal time
Eternity past present and future
I never run out
But time for you to use is slipping away
And in this you must know destiny is calling
And it won't delay
In that obey my commands for...

I AM GOD THE FATHER
AND LOVE WITHOUT CONDITION

I find my pleasure in you
No matter your color or position
No matter where you are or where you have been
Step into my love just as you are
Come

My children, I Am God the Father, and I love you without condition. I find pleasure in you no matter your color or position.

As you walk with me and talk with me, I tell you that you are my own. It is not my purpose to cause confusion to your soul. No, it is for me to heal, deliver, and make you whole.

I intend to shake all that can be shaken until the things of me are the only things standing. Be still in those seasons, and know that I Am God the Father and I love you without condition. I find pleasure in you no matter your color or position.

I desire to gently lay my head upon yours and transfer my thoughts about the way I see you as my sons and daughters. You are heirs to my eternal throne. You are welcome in my eternal home. My door is always open.

My thoughts about you are for good not evil, a future, and hope, freedom, healing, deliverance, and wholeness.

I nurture you with understanding and joy.

My gifts to you are peace, faithfulness, and unfailing love.

Responsibility and accountability are prerequisites for a wonderful future and destiny fulfilled.

My plan is eternal, and my plan has always been.

Know the thoughts I think about you are for you, not against. They outnumber the grains of the sand upon the seashores from the beginning to the end of which has always been and always will be, for I Am eternal and eternity is me.

I cherish every thought of you. I love you just the way you are.

When you walk through times of despair, I Am there amidst you. When the winds blow, hold on tight. I have a pad to land.

When the leaves swirl with twisted lies and the dirt of the world and the stones of accusation and temptation pelt your soul, endure with patience according to faith in what I speak, not what you see.

Be assured, I steady your steps and lift you to myself and embrace you with compassion and long-suffering.

In the silent hours, listen with the ears of your heart. The beat of mine will transform yours.

My gentle whisper validates you are my wonderful creation. I knit you in your mother's womb. I fashioned and formed you and know when you sit and stand. I know the words you are going to speak before one of them is said.

You are the image of my Son and worth my life that I gave. You don't have to change a thing for me to open my arms so you can jump in.

Open the eyes of your understanding. Allow me to speak a revelation of who I created you to be. Fear not. I'll plant you in the garden in which you are to grow. Angels will tend your vines. Nations will eat of your fruit.

You are my songs of love. I sang them into you. The world needs to hear you.

I cherish your adoration and thanksgiving. They are sweet fragrances within the aroma of heaven.

I Am your protection and ever-present help in time of need even though circumstances say I Am not.

Dream big. Shoot for the stars. Live in my love just as you are.

I adopt you as my own. I nurture you as my heart. I protect you as my crown.

You are my joy and imagination. You are like the heavens with my glory and design. You are the strands in the fabric of my plan.

Does the rain have a father
Whose power holds the drops of dew
Is forever my eternal plan
Do the flowers have their fragrance
Apart from my command
Does my voice whisper to the sea
Do you know I Am the freedom you seek

I Am God the Father
And love without condition
I find my pleasure in you
No matter your color or position

I Am God the Father
Please dream big my children
Shoot for the stars

And live in my love just as you are

Am I the beat of your heart
Do my thoughts capture your mind
Do you know
You are like the heavens
With my glory and design
I created every cell of your life
Like the mystery of the wind and time

I Am God the Father
And love without condition
I find my pleasure in you
No matter your color or position

I Am God the Father
Please dream big my children
Shoot for the stars

And live in my love just as you are

Don't you know how special you are
When you capture my heart
And I desire your love
And I gave all that I Am to give you my name
My identity is yours to take

My children you are not a mistake
You are my best creation
And I Am proud to be your Dad in heaven

I long for you to know and hear
My sweet sound to you as your heavenly Father
To you as my beloved sons and daughters

Please look at my Son
And prove His heart
He is the only one
That paid the price no one else could

He is the one and only sacrifice
That has ever been...

CRUCIFIED
AND ROSE AGAIN SO YOU CAN LIVE

I have been crucified for you
And by leaving me out of your life
You live as if you don't know

You live as if you don't know
I Am eternal freedom ringing
And salvation for your soul

My children, there are times when it seems easy for you to see me. There are also times of ease when it is easy to believe and the answers are there before your prayer. However, there are times when the waters of life rise and the dryness of wilderness seasons attempt to blind you to who I Am and what I've done.

I Am that I Am, and I Am Almighty God. I Am eternity from the beginning to the end that never will be and never has been.

I Am the truth, and the truth is me. And I Am amidst you now healing my truth and exposing the world's unbelief.

It matters not what you believe. It changes not the truth that I Am who I say that I Am.

My blood was poured out to purchase your soul. My will was given up so you could be my very own.

How easily it is to forget the price I paid. Rampant is the wavering with no thought of the fee upon my head. It wasn't a crown of jewels that graced my brow. It was the crown of thorns shrouding my dignity marring me with humility and disgrace. Please consider.

Do you even really care?

Oh, how easy is it to forget the cross because I Am on the other side. Consider the cross as the weapon that opened the door to my resurrection and your salvation.

I Am amidst you now healing my truth so the lie will be found out.

The truth is I paid the price no one else could.

I overcame the grave, suffered the shame, wore the pain, took on humility's face, offered my spirit in faith, gave up my will for my Father's instead, and loved you to the grave and rose again.

The truth is I spared nothing for your sake.

Perhaps you will take my offer in your heart's embrace. Remember, I gave my life so yours could be saved.

The truth is I forgive you anyway.

Can't you see me crying? It may look as though the sun is shining oh so bright when really I Am crucified over and over again by the way you live with disregard for my love.

There are times when it seems easy
For you to see me
And recognize I Am the Lord
And Savior of your lives
When life is going well
And the answers are already there
Before you ever finish your precious prayer

How easily it is to forget my undying love
And how I gave you life all along
When things don't go as planned
And you can't figure out why

You live as if you're angry
When your will isn't the one I grant
You seem to mock
The very hand that feeds
When you don't realize
It was me that was crucified all along

Why do you complain
And spit in my face
When the seasons don't fall
Within reasoning's grace
Or time doesn't move at your command
My children I hear your cries
And I see your tears roll
Please don't forget
I was the one that took the fall

I see your busyness
And lack of interest in me
But I still keep knocking on your heart
As if it were eternity

I see the indifference and the despondency
When things don't go your way
Because you don't trust me
You trust in other things

Can't you hear my cries
Don't you feel my tears

I see you running to and fro without a thought of me
I see you figuring out and reasoning my plan

Can't you see me from there
I can see you from here
And what I see

Is perhaps you don't really care

You live your life
As if the sun is shining
Oh so bright
And the sky is bright sparkling blue
Like the crystal ocean waves
And a baby's first adoring glance

I can tell you true
I see you live your life
And I stand by wanting for you to understand
That as you live with no regard for my plan

You crucify my heart over and over again

As my tears fall from the bright blue sky
You may think
The sun is shining oh so bright
When really

I've just been crucified over and over again

You live as if you don't know
That I have sorrow too
I watch your life just pass you by
Too proud to know I have feelings also

I see your pain
Can't you see mine

Or do you even care

Don't you know I Am eternal
And I Am forever God
And my love I won't withdraw
That's on your part

Why do you turn the other way
Afraid someone might see
That I Am in your every cell
And it's not by chance or luck that destiny is revealed
But by every word
That comes from my heart

I Am that I Am, and I Am the truth come to set you free. The truth is, I Am really the truth you seek, and I Am your own destiny.

Listen, my children, my plans are the ones that succeed. Surrender your will for mine. I surrendered my will for my Father in kind.

I have your best interest in my heart. Don't push me away. I Am your hope, and hope is me. I Am here and won't ever leave.

Don't you know when you hold to your plans and not mine, I cry for you, my children?

My destiny cost me more than you'll ever know. You were the joy set before me, so I carried my cross proudly and I accomplished more...

MORE THAN YOU'LL EVER KNOW
BECAUSE I WAS CREATED
TO TAKE YOUR PLACE

It was my call
And it was my soul to bare your pain
It was my purpose to pour out my blood
So yours could be saved

If you put me on the throne
And realize
I Am amidst you now healing my truth
You will understand
What I did for you is more than you'll ever know

My children, do you know the pain I lived and the gain you were given that day I stood in the darkness of the world on my cross?

Do you understand I lived your loss? Do you know my Father saw your sin and poured it upon me? I gladly bore it. Did I not?

Have you ever felt the warmth of my blood on your face as you sit alone in your desperate state?

Where is your cross? Do you carry it daily? Do you hold it stately as you march in faith? I did so that one day you would have the strength to do the same.

Where is your heart? Is it in fear?

Where is your mind? Is it sheltered in dread?

Where are your trembling feet if they aren't walking with me? Are they in fear's grip of agony?

Can you imagine the cost that I paid?

Can you fathom the depth of my grave?

Can you handle the truth that I speak?

I Am the truth and the truth is me. And the truth is I've come to set you free.

Where have I called you?

Where does your soul roam?

What is your purpose? What is your plan? Are you willing for mine to be put in your hand?

I Am amidst you now healing my truth the darkness tried to usurp.

I Am the Light of the world and always have been and forever will be. You are my image and the light the world sees.

It cost me more than you'll ever know
To see your sin
To bare your sin and live your loss
As I stood inexorably entwined in all the darkness
Of the world on my cross that day

It was my call
It was my soul so yours could be saved
It was my heart on display

Where is your cross
Do you carry it daily
Do you wear it stately as you march in faith
Or is it fear that you walk in

Do you walk in trepidation allowing the timid to remain
Or do you trust in me and call on my name

Do you walk in the present shedding the past
Where there is freedom
And an unlimited future

Do you drown in your sorrow
Or dwell in my presence where there is fullness of joy

Do you cast your bread upon the water
If you do it will return cleansed

And you will be my redemption story

Do you look to me for your strength
And live in the radiance of the Father I Am
Do you delight yourself in me
And receive your heart's desires

Do you trust me in times of trouble
If you do I will rescue you
And you will be the display of my glory

I find pleasure in you my son and my daughter
And I Am honored to reward you
With blessing in your soul

As you love me
Your soul will be rich with life and peace
Your heart will find healing from every kind of strife

Your mind will be nourished with food from my feast
And your life will shine like the stars in the universe

You will reap the harvest of a light drawn path
And the blessing of fulfilling the destiny of my plans
And if you fulfill the destiny of my plans
You will be filled with joy
You can't find in any other land

You will know what it is to carry your cross daily
And you will understand how to wear your cross stately

You will share in the fellowship of my sufferings

But in turn

You will live your life in the power of my resurrection
With that in mind...

WILL YOU WAIT ON ME
FOR I AM YOUR KING

Will you wait on me
During the times of hardship
As well as
During the times of plenty

Will you wait on me
When the gates of hell knock upon your door
And the darkened trials set courage to flight

Will you wait on me
When loss and confusion tap into your life

Will you wait on me
In the seasons of patient enduring

Will you wait on me
For everything

My children, if you wait on me for everything, you will renew your strength. Be still and know that I Am God. You will mount up with wings like eagles high above your circumstances, problems, failure, success, joy, sorrow, sowing, reaping, strength, weakness, or what other people think.

When the gates of hell knock at the door of your courage and faith, my truth can set you free. Wait on me and you will see.

When confusion is ushered into the depths of your soul, know my Spirit isn't bound by confusion or anything the darkness conjures.

Will you wait on me when you can't stand another negative, harmful thing pulling at your heartstrings?

Listen for my voice. Wait on me until you hear it. Do not follow the echo of deceit.

Wait on my Spirit to move and lead you into all truth. I Am that I Am, and I Am your solution. I Am the truth you seek, and the truth is me.

I Am amidst you now healing my truth, and I desire to bring each of you to the end of yourself. When you are finally there, questions will always appear. They will chart your course.

Will you wait on me?

Will you allow me to be your God?

Is my Spirit your counselor?

Do you trust my peace to be the governor of your heart?

Is my presence the fullness of your joy?

Does my instruction lead you to a fulfilled life? It should.

Will the kingdom of this world pull you to the outer ends of the darkness, beyond the pale where hardness of heart becomes your enemy, pretending to be your protection and friend?

It is imperative for you to know it is by my Spirit that worthy things are done.

It is in trusting obedience where life is truly won.

Captives are set free and my victory is set in stone when I Am the voice you heed and the rock you stand upon.

Do not be fooled. I Am amidst you now healing my truth that I Am the one true God. It doesn't matter if you believe it or not. My truth will withstand all your doubt.

Lies last for the moment, but truth stands the test of time. Test and try me.

I know it's easier to believe a lie because truth brings accountability that makes the fainthearted want to run and hide. Accountability calls responsibility to run its course. Responsibility is difficult to swallow sometimes.

You will discover if you wait on me, I won't ever fail, leave, or forsake you.

If you wait upon me
You will renew your strength
And mount up with wings like eagles

The question is my children

Will you wait on me

Will you wait when the gates of hell
Knock upon your door

Will you wait when the trials surpass the courage you have

Will you wait when the liberty of my Spirit
Is in question

Will you wait when confusion pushes
Into the entrance to your soul

Will you wait when you can't stand
Another pressing thing

Will you wait when your heart
Is not only breaking
But when your heart is at last
And finally broken

Will you then listen to my voice

Will you lay aside your own ways
And your own thoughts
And trust as the heavens are high above the earth
So are my ways
And it is also thus my thoughts

If you can but wait on me
On my Spirit and rejoice
It will be perfected in you to know
That it is by my Spirit things are done
It is by your trusting obedience life is won
Captives are set free and my victory set in stone

This I say to you my children
My overcoming ones
Please wait on me when you think I Am not around

Will you wait on me when the world shouts
With all its deceit
And when every other sound takes the place of me
And the truth I Am

Will you wait on me as your king
When power fame and fortune wear the world's crown
And not me at all

Will you wait on me as your God
When the world esteems me as foolish
And an old fable or fantasy story

Will you wait on me and...

LOOK NOT
TO THE MOUNTAINS OR THE HILLS

Look not to the mountains or the hills
For your hand to touch mine

For I Am amidst you now healing my truth
And I Am the truth and the truth is me
Don't you know my truth is the freedom you seek

Look not to the darkness of the world
To illuminate your path
For I Am the Light of the world
And The Light of the world is me

And you cannot see the steps to freedom
In the darkness you see

But I the Light of the world
Shine upon your true self
And lead you into the destiny I breath

My children, look not to the mountains or the hills for your hand to touch mine.

Look not to the east or the west, gold, silver, idols, or vain things to be the gods you serve.

Look to me and my miracles to perform. Take me for who I Am because I Am God, on your behalf to adorn.

Don't sacrifice yourself for earthly gain. Don't sacrifice your joy for unholy fame. Do not seek after vainglory or riches that won't sustain. Look not to what doesn't matter in the end.

Sacrifice not your peace when traveling life's journey. Do not listen to the voice of a stranger.

Give me your heart and your best. Choose me in life's pressure and journey.

Look not to the mountains or the hills for your hope. I created the mountains and spoke existence into the hills. I gave the springtime its flowers and clothed the winter with chill. I sprayed the aroma of fall on the fading summer sun. I created the masterpiece of the stars and set the moon in its home. I cradled the new day born in the stillness of my calm. I gave the birds their song and the honeybee its comb. When there were no oceans, I gave wisdom its birth. My understanding established the heavens beyond the limitation of mankind.

Look not to the mountains or the hills for your redemption. When there were no springs abounding with water or mountains settled in place, my wisdom was the hand that held the sky in its place. Before the hills found their resting place, my grace established its boundaries for you to partake. And my boundaries fall to you in pleasant places for your protection.

Look not to the mountains or the hills for your provision. Look to my faithfulness because it reaches beyond the sky. Walk in the way of righteousness along my paths of justice where I bestow my wealth on those who love me and make their treasuries full.

I will bring all of you, my children, to the end of yourself. You will be faced with the issue of where your hope will discover itself.

If you look to the mountains and the hills with pride and arrogance as your guide, you will be sorely disappointed. Counsel and sound judgment are what you will hear from me.

Look not to the mountains or the hills to bring you forth, but look to me. I Am the master craftsman.

Look not to the pottery for your strength but to the potter whose muscles fashioned and formed the earth.

Be careful not to sacrifice your hearts and souls for the emptiness of what the world holds. Vanity brings hollowness to your days. If you seek your own glory, fame, and fortune without a thought of my ways, you will find your heart desolate and your soul staring in space.

Have I mentioned your sons and daughters? Do not sacrifice them so you can do your own thing. If you do, time will have a way of finding you and eat at your hours as quick as they come.

When will you learn it's not the mountains or the hills, the streams or the fields, fame or fortune, the gold or silver, cattle on a thousand hills, diamonds and rubies, the universe or stars, power and possessions, beauty or charm, but me that performs miracles and displays my glory that confounds the proud?

I Am that I Am Almighty God, the master craftsman of the universe, establishing galaxies and time.

Do not depend on what I create. Depend on me.

My children look not to the east or the west
Look not to gold or silver
Not to idols and vain things
But look to me my miracles to perform

Look about you
Can you not see my blessings overflowing
And feel my heart throbbing

Look not to the mountains and hills
Look not to the sacrifice and burnt offerings

But look to me my miracles to perform

I Am God
There is none other
Only believe
But be sure to believe in me

For it is in me the Lord
Where your storehouse of treasure is released

Look not to the earthly heathen altars
Sacrifice not your sons and daughters
Idol worship is an abomination in my sight

Look not to yourself
Nor your own wisdom to replace mine

Seek my face and listen
It is not in the sun moon or the stars
You find your strength

It is not in the mountains and hills
Your reach will meet my hand
But it is in my word on bended knee before me as your king
Humble in your asking
Patient in your receiving
Walking with my Spirit side by side with me
Obeying every word as I speak

Isn't that what I did
I did just what the Father said

And followed in His steps
Hearing what He thought
Doing what He said
And finding my nourishment
From every word that came out of His mouth

Then doing His will to the end

Are you not supposed to do the same
And follow in my steps

Trusting I will take care of all your needs
And restore what has been lost

Look not to the east or west to fulfill your desires
Or the swift winter chill to put out your fires
Or the bursting forth of spring to save your family

Look to me for everything

I was rejected by my own
But I Am precious to God my Father
Who chose me to be His Son
And the chief cornerstone
And stumbling block to the naysayers

If you look to me with trust
You will never be disappointed
I Am the solution to your every need
Problem or mistake so...

FEAR NOT MISTAKES
I USE THEM TO SET
HEAVEN IN PLACE

Do you know
I Am amidst you now
Not to condemn but to forgive

Do you know
I Am amidst you now healing my truth

And what is my truth
I Am my truth and the truth is me
And I say the truth is
Fear not mistakes

My children, fear not mistakes. As they come, let them go. Learn from them before they leave you though. With my understanding as your friend, mistakes can be used to set heaven in your midst.

Forgiveness is the key to the door of heaven's bliss, and I Am the door and the key all at once.

Do you view your mistakes as a mistake or a chance to be covered in my grace? Don't justify mistakes and take advantage of the forgiveness I died to give. Take hold of my love that gives allowance for your faults.

Fear not mistakes. Learn from them. Love them in their proper place. I can use your mistakes, touch their weakness with my strength, and bring glory to my name.

Fear not mistakes always and forever. Look not upon your faults and weakness as your gods. Look to me and my miracles to perform. Look into my blood, and you will see my love.

Look upon my face and my beaded brow. Feel my bruised body and my broken heart. If you do, you won't fear mistakes. You'll understand if you allow me the chance. You'll see my love and feel the arms of my compassion in your faults.

Fear not mistakes. Allow me to use them as tools to mold and shape. Let them be opportunities to love you and cause you to draw near to who I Am.

I Am amidst you now healing my truth. The truth is, I know who you are. You are my child. I know that for sure. I expect you to walk imperfectly before you run steady and strong. Then you'll run and not grow weary as you depend on me. You'll walk and not faint mounting up with wings like eagles as you trust me for everything.

I Am amidst you now healing my truth that I have given you power, love, and a sound mind. Fear is not me and never has been nor ever will be. I Am that I Am forever your peace.

Condemnation is not what I give. Conviction is a much better way. So fear not mistakes. Look at things a different way.

Was it a mistake
Or allowance covered with my grace

With my understanding
Mistakes can set heaven in place

Fear not mistakes
They can be turned my wisdom
And used to shape your world

Fear not mistakes
Learn from them instead
Love them in their proper place
For is not your sin what I forgive

Is not your shame my opportunity
For my glory to reign
And healing to take its place

Yes my children fear not mistakes
Human imperfection is what I overcame

Was it a mistake for me to shed my blood

I dare not think so
It was my love

So look upon your faults
Upon your weakness my strength to perform

Look into my blood and you will see my love
In its splendid majesty and form
Look upon my face
My beaded brow
My bruised body
My broken heart
And you will fear not mistakes

For if you understand you will see my love
Feel my arms and welcome my touch

Yes fear not mistakes
I allow them you know

You are my children I know that so well

Fear not mistakes
As they come let them go

Allow me to use them to shape and to mold
To transform what is into what I have in store

So fear not mistakes
I know who you are

You are my children
I expect you not to run before you walk

I love you still mistakes and all

So are they mistakes
Or allowances covered with my grace
And my chance to show you forgiveness instead

Fear not mistakes
Simply live in my grace
Do not remain in your chains
Do not make my death be in vain
Live in my freedom and be not a...

PRISON CHILD
CRYING OVER THERE

Prison child in all walks of life
Do you know I see you and your invisible tears

Do you know I hear you and your searing pain

Do you know I Am faithful
Within the chains you are bound

Prison child crying with no tears. I hear your heart writhing with the wind. The ebb and flow of the beating of crime doesn't stop my hand from forgiving and easing your mind.

Prison child lost in confusion, enslaved in fear's embrace. I tell you I Am amidst you now to calm your heart. Seek not strife to take the place of the peace that's at stake.

Prison child with walls all around. I ask you to come and I will be found. Draw near to my heart, and I will draw near to yours. Seek my presence in the midst of your doubt.

Prison child entangled in the lies. Come to me with a pure heart inside. You will be blessed. Your chains will be released, and true freedom will be what I give in the place of defeat.

Prison child wallowing in shame, living in locked down cells of cement and mortar in your soul. Know I lived your sorrow, felt your pain, died in its place, and rose again from the grave.

Prison child, I have walked your lonely road. My crown of thorns couldn't keep me down. I Am here to release you from prison and draw you home.

Prison child in your three-piece suit. I see you running through the streets with a briefcase in hand, chasing after winds of success, striving to live up to the pedestal others have put you on. There's no need for that with me. Be free. Come down.

Prison child straining to be a supermom. Depend on me for your strength, and I will lead you in all things. Pour my Spirit into your sons and teach your daughters of me above all. Know indulgence is not your burden nor is it your call.

Prison child laboring to be a dad. I notice. I see you working hours and days on end to satisfy your family even though they neglect your feelings and don't appreciate your effort. I hear your heart and know you desire to give them more than you ever had.

Sometimes it would be easy to think that I Am a Father because nothing hurts more than being a mother; however, there is no greater hurt than to put your own son on the cross and turn the other way, especially if your son was freely given for someone who would just as soon delete Him from existence, murder His love, shame His grace, hate who He is, and deny that He ever came. Won't you break the chains and enjoy the life my Son died to give?

Prison child reaching for the stars. Go ahead and dream of all that you are. If all that you are is in me, you will come to life and find all you'll ever need.

Prison child starving yourself to death. Don't you know you're fearfully and wonderfully made, and you're beautiful to me? No one else can take your place.

Prison child treading the mill of the world's ways, making money hand over fist. Know I felt your emptiness when I was in the grave. That's why I didn't remain there. I had to rise again so you can be saved.

Prison child living above your means and below the person you are meant to be. I overcame so you didn't have to live to impress others. I call you victorious over life's riches that once obtained can become an affliction to your soul if they are what you love above anything or anyone else or me as God.

Prison child be who I created you to be. You're not a puppet on a string. Do all I created you to do. And remember, laziness ends in slave labor and makes the rafters sag.

Prison child, rejoice in who I Am. Embrace my every word. Acknowledge me as God. Honor me as your heavenly Father. Heed my voice and pave the way for my coming with yours. Follow and seek me above all else.

Prison child with your scarred face. Don't worry. I hold you in my embrace.

Prison child, if you fall short of the world's standards, be not dismayed. The world didn't accept me either.

Prison child destitute and shaken. Worry not. I Am your sustenance, and you'll never be forsaken.

Prison child ranging to and fro. Stop. Listen. Follow my instructions. They lead you to a fulfilled life.

Prison child stricken with failure. There is no failure in me.

Prison child betrayed by those you give your life. Fret not. Was I not betrayed the same?

Grieve no more. Justice is my name. When the thief is caught, he has to repay.

Prison child lost and forsaken. Call out to me. I know every hair on your head.

Prison child oversized and hiding. I see you over there. Beauty is not the outward but the inward person of the heart. Do you love me pure, or do you not? That is what I judge, is it not?

Prison child deformed and chided. I knew you before your mother's womb. I loved you then more than you will ever know, and I love you now just like you are.

Prison child living in abuse. I see you even though you think I do not. I love you and will never leave or forsake you. The world does, but I Am not the world and its abusive ways.

I Am that I Am, and I Am love ever healing and love ever giving life, abundant with a future and a hope of good and not evil. Test me. Prove me out.

Prison child fighting with all your worth. I not only won the battles, but I won the war.

Prison child, I Am here to save you. I Am not your dad or mom who left you to fend for yourself.

Prison child screaming in your corner of pain. I saw you when your daddy molested you and when your momma gave you shame. I saw the next-door neighbor when he broke your windowpane and held you at gunpoint, stealing your virginity away.

Prison child, I saw your happiness slither away when your teacher made fun of you in front of your peers. I Am not blind to your streams of tears. I have come to wipe them from you and give you new eyes to see. I have come to nurture your soul and lift you from despair.

Prison child, I see the bullies on their pride-studded throne. Don't you worry about their injustice though. My justice balances the scale.

Prison child crying over there. I saw you when you were only twelve and daddy left the house. He never came back, but I Am always around. I Am proud to give you my name and sit you on my lap and hold you near my heart.

Prison child, I saw you when your mother had a breakdown because life was just too much. You thought no one was there, but I was hanging out. Call on me now, and you will see I Am here to help and set your hurting heart free.

Prison child orphaned and alone. I know your anguish and insecurity, and I Am here to call you my own.

Prison child living in the past. Stop! Come into the irresistible present I have for you to dwell.

Prison child suffering for the truth. Stay your course, and call evil to account.

Prison child, addiction isn't where I have for you to live. A miracle is what you need. I give them daily. I have one for you. Be not afraid.

Prison child always in the way. Know that I Am amidst you now and want you to come and play.

Prison child in the sunset of your life. You feel as if you are a burden and worthless even though you hold the keys to wisdom the school of life has birthed. Life and others make you feel you have nothing to offer and there is nothing for you to do. But I tell you that you are my greatest stories that I want told as a garland to grace the earth. Please don't fear. Know as long as you have breath, I have things for you to do.

Prison child never right but wrong. I see your efforts to help your family along. Sometimes children can be hard, and they can hurt more than you can bare, but know you are my children, and I Am your heavenly Dad.

You hurt me sometimes more than I convey. That's why I sent my precious Son to share my forgiving way. If I didn't send him as the sacrifice, no one would have cared as much as me to want you as their next of kin and precious family.

Prison child living in the past. Let it go! I Am here to usher you into your unlimited future showered in hope.

Prison child who doesn't understand when no one seems to care. I see you knocking on the door of hearts, trying to get them to respond. It makes you feel like you have to beg, but I Am always here even if you think I Am not.

Well here I Am knocking on the door of your heart and tugging from above. All I want is to give you life and set you free from the prisons that hold you captive. Please respond.

Prison child I see you in the corner all alone
Your eyes as the doe
And your heart as a fawn

Know I Am for you not against

Prison child writhing in your pain
Wallowing in the mud slippery and wet

I see your eyes crying with no tears
Too much pain to capture through the years

I hear your heart torn with the wind
And feel your soul untouched by true felt love

I see your shame pain will not forget
Know I died to give you joy
And erase the stain defilement paints

Don't you know I lived your sorrow
On the road to my cross that day

Won't you find me out
And give me a chance to shower you in my grace

Won't you choose me over any other god

Prison child I have walked your lonely road
In my crown of thorns
And I Am with you as you sit in your prison cell
Locked down and alone

I Am that I Am
And I see all that I have planned
I Am Savior and Lord

So I want you to know I cried those tears
You can't seem to face

And I hold the keys to heaven's place
I lived your sorrow hidden as a candle lit
But I Am that I Am the Light of the world

Prison child you can be free
If you choose to be
Because I Am that I Am
And I Am the freedom you seek

Cast aside your pride and give me a try
I Am that I Am forgiveness and I will never hide

Look into my face and you will see
I Am looking back at you with eternal love forgiving
I paid the ultimate fee

Prison child enslaved in man's judgment
Fear your chattering feet

Know condemnation is not the word I speak

Conviction is from me
And I Am that I Am
And I Am forgiveness don't you see

I Am many things
But you need to know
I Am amidst you now healing my truth
That I Am not dead...

I AM ALIVE AND RISEN
AND HERALD MY TRUTH

My children what do you believe

Do you believe the lie
That I Am dead
Or do you believe the truth
That I Am alive and I Am risen

I Am amidst you now healing my truth

I Am that I Am
And I Am the truth and the truth is me

The truth is I Am not in the grave powerlessly bound to chains

I Am alive and I Am risen

Am amidst you now healing my truth. And the truth is I Am very much alive, and I herald my voice though you think I Am silent.

Mankind has thought of me as of no effect and never have been, but I Am that I Am, and I Am Almighty God and always will be.

I say again and again that I Am bringing each of you, my children, to the end of yourself. At the end of yourself, you will discover some questions.

Who will you choose this day? Will it be me, or will it be false gods or the world's system or your own way?

After you have answered those questions, there will be more.

Will you lay down your life for mine?

Will you take my plan and give yours into my hand?

Will you trust my unfailing love reaching to the heavens?

Will you lean on my faithfulness that is new every morning?

Will you cast aside pride and live in humble dependence?

Will you panic when all things that can be shaken are shaken?

Will you understand when evil is exposed and brought to account?

Will you accept responsibility on freedom's behalf?

Will you live in faith knowing that all things hidden will come to light?

Will you cry out to me and make me your refuge and strength?

Will you hold my hand as you walk through the fires of oppression?

Will you swim against the current and eventually drown, or will you flow in the river of my blessings, obedient to my will?

The choice is yours. You can live in the lie that I Am dead, or you can ask me into your heart and believe that I Am the only power of true deliverance, complete joy, whole fulfillment, absolute release, and total healing and freedom.

I Am your ever-present help in time of trouble. I Am all you'll ever need. Where will you turn when the earth gives way and the mountains fall into the sea? You will know in that moment a dead god will not be your rescuing power.

Though the oceans of life roar and the waters of insecurity foam and the mountains of upset quake, be still and know that I Am the ultimate life preserver.

Though pools of confused emotions bellow inside your soul, know I Am not dead. I Am alive, and I Am risen!

Though an avalanche of problems seeks to take over your ability to fight and overcome, though heartache trembles in each and every step, you must know I Am bigger.

Though nations are in an uproar and kingdoms fall, you must know I Am on the throne. Fear not.

Though the sky is falling around the dreams of your goals, though temptation offers a better resolve, though tempests and storms toss you to and fro, be still and know that I Am God.

Though you think the wicked rule and deception controls the mind of the world, though waterfalls of rage pummel and the seeming absence of me is all about, be still and know that I Am active and thriving on your account.

Though distraught and distraction play the same tune
And there's made little room for me in the midst of life's doom

Though man will fail and disappoint
And your tears fall through the night
Know I Am in position I Am not dead

I Am alive and I Am risen

Though you think of me silent
I Am not

Hardness of heart has quenched my voice
But I render my will into my Father's hand
And listen and carry out all His commands

Soon oh so soon my reckoning will be
And no man woman or child
Shall be able to ignore
I Am that I Am

I Am the truth and not the lie

Forsake me not
I will come as a thief in the night

In the night of your sorrow
And confusion that you find
I Am that I Am and I Am God on my throne

In the night of evil
I Am that I Am and I Am the judge
Desiring mercy more than to condemn

In the night of confusion and loss
And the upside down world
I Am that I Am the Father and Son
And wonderful counselor you can depend upon

Though you think I Am not
You can be sure that I Am on the scene
And I know all things big and small and between

I Am the judge of the heart
Man's yardstick is not mine

Though you take from me
And give to the enemy of your soul

Though the lie is easier for now
I Am that I Am and I Am not dead
I Am not bound to the grave

Though multitudes try to remove me from their world
I Am that I Am and I Am the truth

And the truth is I Am not dead
I Am alive and I Am risen

Though you cast me aside as a shameful symbol
I died that you might live

And that you might give your life
As a testimony of my love and overcoming power

My faithfulness is new every morning
My love is unfailing
My presence is fullness of joy
My peace is your reward

And compromise chills your soul

I laid down my life and took it up again
So too my child lay down your life
And I will take it up again

Lay down your ambition and take my plan
Offer a sacrifice of trust
Leave it in my hands

I Am faithfulness to your heart
Healing love and the cross

I Am believing when you cannot see
I Am the beginning and the end
Eternity if you please

I Am the rock of ages you can stand upon
I Am the first fruit of those born from the dead

Fear not
Be not dismayed or discouraged any longer

Hope always in my unfailing love
I Am not still hanging on the cross
I Am seated at the right hand of my Father

Allow me to take your mind heart will
And emotions there with me
Where there is honor power splendor favor and grace

Oh my children
I have always loved you and I always will

Come with me now
Come with me always

Allow me to show you
The power of love and death overcome
And the joy of victory of the Father's beloved Son
To you my beloved ones

Test me
Try me
I will prove myself

SECTION THREE

My children, I hear you calling. I Am here, ever-present, amidst you now and forever replying.

I say to you, I hate evil and the tolerance of the day. However, I Am forgiveness and won't turn anyone away.

Will you offer anything but forgiveness to your fellow man?

Those without sin, cast the first stone.

This is the time and the season of accounting. You need not account for another. You have need of working out your own salvation with fear and trembling.

As you live, move, and have your being in me, I will go before you and prepare the way. I will hide you underneath the shadow of my wings. Walk with me hand-in-hand. Lean on me with your whole heart, and I will keep you in perfect peace and able to withstand the storms life brings.

Who will you believe? Will you turn to me and trust me with all that you are? If you do, I will give you my joy. I will give you my peace that passes human understanding. I will comfort you with my grace and clothe you with my love. Which way will you turn? Will you turn to the world's ways, your own thinking or to me?

Turn to me and there you will find mercy ever-present. You will discover my faithfulness that reaches to the heavens. My arms will be outstretched, and my voice will lead you on to victory.

The prize of the upward call is your reward.

I Am not dead

I Am alive and I Am risen

You are forgiven!

CPSIA information can be obtained
at www.ICGtesting.com
Printed in the USA
BVHW010306030419

544444BV00004B/5/P